ENGINEERING ANSWERS

Why Arches and Triangles Are Strong

BY MARNE VENTURA

Kids Core
An Imprint of Abdo Publishing
abdobooks.com

abdobooks.com

Published by Abdo Publishing, a division of ABDO, PO Box 398166, Minneapolis, Minnesota 55439.

Printed in the United States of America, North Mankato, Minnesota.
102024
012025

Cover Photo: Shutterstock Images
Interior Photos: Joseph Hendrickson/Shutterstock Images, 4–5; Sean Pavone/Shutterstock Images, 6; Bettmann/Getty Images, 8; Shutterstock Images, 10, 12–13, 16, 18, 20–21, 26, 28 (top), 28 (bottom); Wayne Via/Shutterstock Images, 11; Vaughan Sam/stock Images, 15; Trong Nguyen/Shutterstock Images, 23; Red Line Editorial, 24; iStockphoto, 29 (top); ABC Photos/Shutterstock Images, 29 (bottom)

Editor: Marley Richmond
Series Designer: Laura Kuchar

Library of Congress Control Number: 2024938381

Publisher's Cataloging-in-Publication Data

Names: Ventura, Marne, author.
Title: Why arches and triangles are strong / by Marne Ventura
Description: Minneapolis, Minnesota: ABDO Publishing, 2025 | Series: Engineering answers | Includes online resources and index.
Identifiers: ISBN 9781098295912 (lib. bdg.) | ISBN 9798384916918 (ebook)
Subjects: LCSH: Engineering--Juvenile literature. | Arches--Juvenile literature. | Triangle--Juvenile literature. | Buildings--Design and construction--Juvenile literature. | Architectural engineering--Juvenile literature. | Questions and answers--Juvenile literature. | Engineering design--Juvenile literature.
Classification: DDC 620.1--dc23

CONTENTS

People can ride to the top of the Gateway Arch. From there, they can enjoy great views of Saint Louis.

CHAPTER 1

The Gateway Arch

Ava looked up at the huge silver arch. "It looks taller than the Washington Monument!" she said. Ava and her family were in Saint Louis, Missouri. Ava's parents were **engineers**. The family planned vacations to see famous buildings and structures.

Each leg of the Gateway Arch is a triangle. At the base of each triangle, the sides are 54 feet (16 m) long. They get smaller as the arch rises.

Mom told Ava that the Gateway Arch is the tallest monument in the United States. It stands 630 feet (190 m) tall.

"What keeps it standing?" Ava asked. The arch looked so simple and thin.

Dad explained that arches are strong shapes. The Gateway Arch was also built with triangles. These shapes make the structure sturdy.

Dad asked Ava to find the arches and triangles in the structure. She saw that each leg of the arch had three sides. They were triangles. Dad explained that these triangles were equilateral. Each side was the same length.

As the legs rose, they curved inward. Dad said the shape is an upside-down catenary arch. This is the shape a chain would take if it was held at both ends and hung down.

The Gateway Arch was built in sections. The two sides of the arch were supported across the middle until the final block was placed in 1965.

Ava walked toward the Gateway Arch. She was excited to learn more.

Arches and Triangles

An arch is a curved structure. It is symmetrical. This means the right and the left side are exactly the same. A triangle is a shape with three straight sides. Each pair of sides forms an angle where they meet.

The Gateway to the West

The Gateway Arch stands on the bank of the Mississippi River. The monument was built to honor the city of Saint Louis as the Gateway to the West. Many people traveled through this spot on their way to make their homes in the western United States.

The Arc de Triomphe is another famous arch. It stands in Paris, France, and honors French soldiers.

Arches and triangles are shapes that carry weight well. They are strong and stable. They keep the Gateway Arch standing. Since ancient times, builders have used arches and triangles to build large structures. Bridges, domes, and

Sydney Harbour Bridge is an arched bridge in Australia.

skyscrapers get their strength from arches and triangles. Dams and tunnels also use these strong shapes.

Further Evidence

Look at the website below. Does it give any new evidence to support Chapter One?

Gateway Arch

abdocorelibrary.com/arches-and-triangles-strong

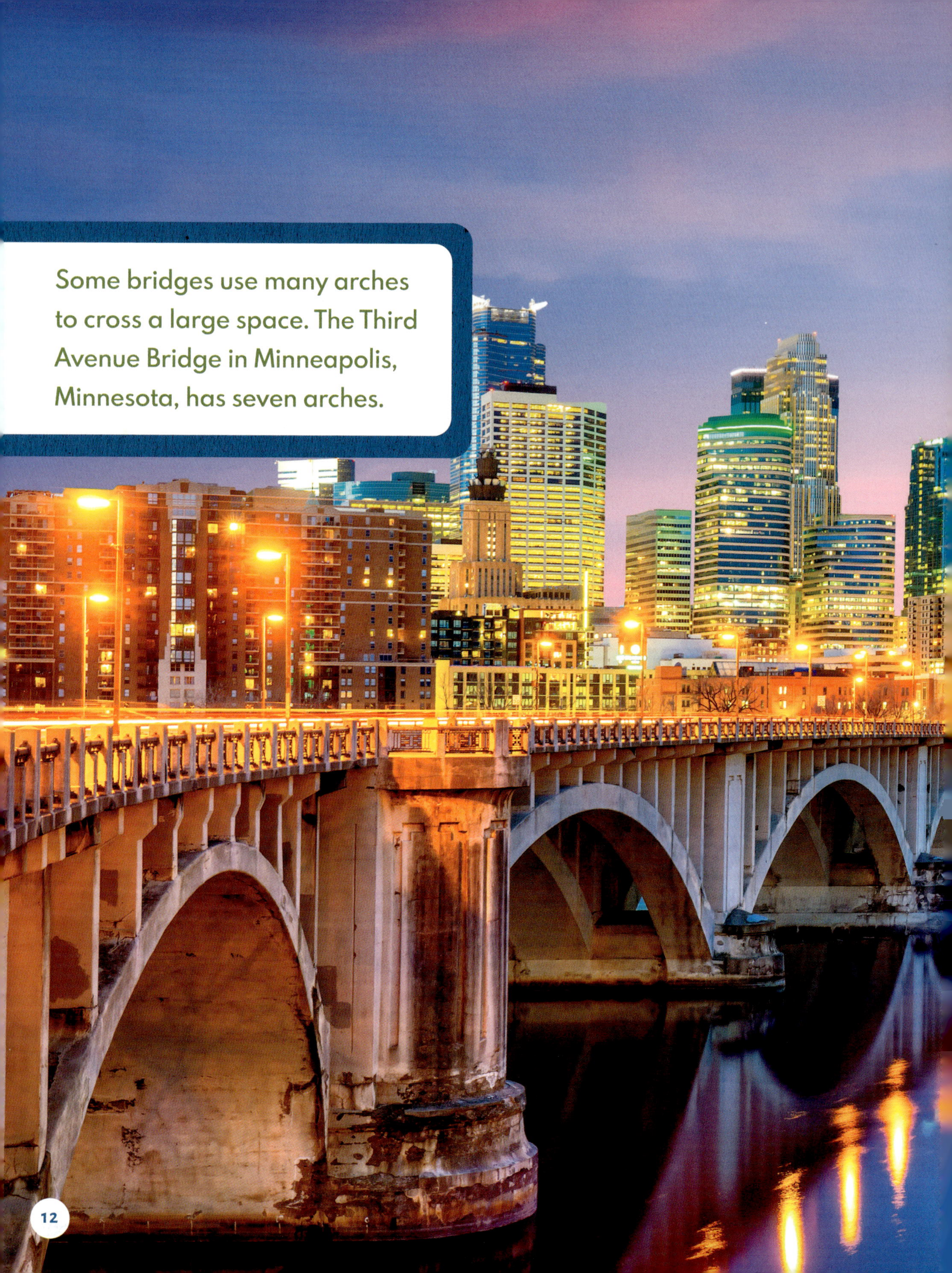

Some bridges use many arches to cross a large space. The Third Avenue Bridge in Minneapolis, Minnesota, has seven arches.

Strong Arches

Builders use arches to **span** openings. Arched bridges cross rivers. An arch in a building might span a window or door. These arches support load. Load is the weight on a structure. Arches can carry more weight than a straight **beam** that spans an opening.

Many arches are made up of wedge-shaped blocks. The upper edge of the block is wider than the lower edge. Blocks are set together side by side to form a curve. The top center block is called the keystone. It holds the rest of the blocks in place, even when weight presses down on it. These blocks are also easier to carry and move into place than long beams.

Roman Arches

Ancient Rome existed more than 2,000 years ago. Ancient Romans used stone arches to build bridges and buildings. Most Roman arches did not use any material to hold the stones together. Their shape and weight held them in place.

Many arches still stand in ancient ruins. These structures are strong enough to stand tall over long periods of time.

Why Arches Are Strong

Arches get their strength from their shape. When a truck drives across a bridge, the weight of the truck pushes down on the arch underneath it.

Strong arches form in nature. Visitors can see more than 2,000 natural arches at Arches National Park in Utah.

The weight causes the material of the arch to squeeze together. This is called compression. Compression gives an arch its strength.

When two objects press against each other, they both apply **force**. These forces are equal in strength. But they push in opposite directions. Equal and opposite forces give structures strength. Engineers use this idea to build strong arches.

Arches spread weight along their curves and down their support posts. This is called transfer. Many arch support posts transfer load into the ground. The ground pushes back. These forces push against each other. They hold the arch steady.

Arch dams use compression and transfer to hold back the force of flowing rivers.

Some dams are built in arched shapes. The sides of a dam's arch are buried deep in rock. Water pushes against the curved dam. The dam transfers this force along the arch and into rock. The rock pushes back. The dam stands strong.

Primary Source

Chad Orzel is a physics professor. He explained how ancient Roman arches stayed strong:

> As gravity pulls the keystone down, it presses into the blocks to either side, exerting a force on them, and they press back with an equal and opposite force. All . . . these forces . . . keep the arch stable.

Source: "The Physics of Ancient Roman Architecture." *Forbes*, 5 July 2016, forbes.com. Accessed 31 May 2024.

Comparing Texts

Think about the quote. Does it support the information in this chapter? Or does it give a different perspective? Explain how in a few sentences.

Pyramids are structures that get their strength from four triangle-shaped sides.

CHAPTER 3

Sturdy Triangles

A polygon is a flat shape with three or more sides. Triangles, rectangles, and squares are polygons. A triangle is the strongest polygon.

Imagine four pieces of wood are joined to form a rectangle.

If each piece was joined with a **hinge**, this shape would be weak. When weight pushes against a corner, the sides would move. The rectangle would flatten out into a diamond shape. But triangles do not change shape when weight pushes on a corner. They stay stiff.

Why Triangles Are Strong

Triangles are strong because they share weight evenly among their three sides. People often use triangles to create strong structures. Engineers design many house roofs in the shape of triangles.

Forces such as gravity push against the roof. The roof transfers this load down two sides of the triangle. The two sides squeeze down.

Builders use triangle shapes when creating the structure for many buildings. These shapes keep buildings strong.

Structural Forces

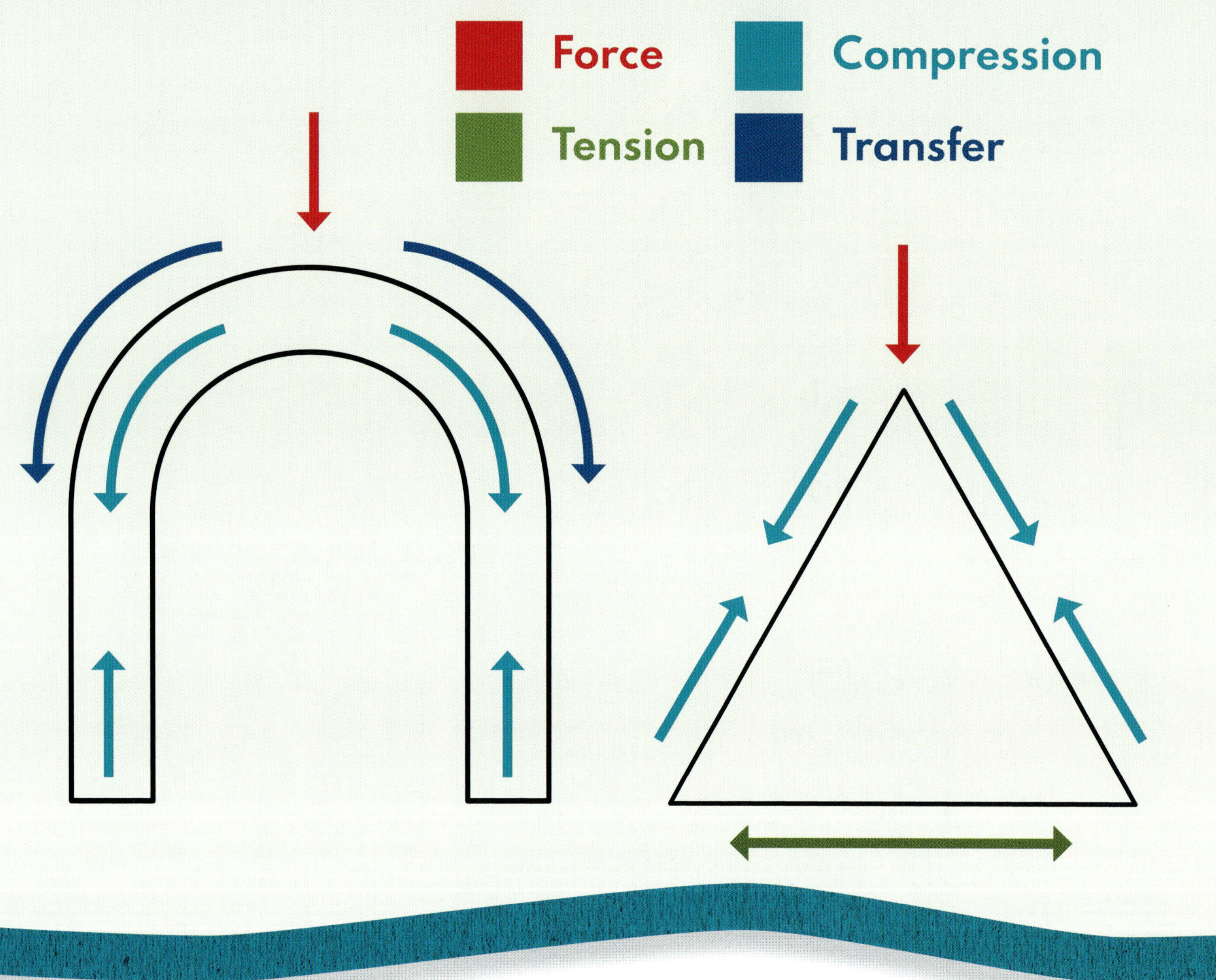

Equal compression and tension allow triangles to hold strong under pressure. Compression and transfer hold arches steady.

They compress. This pulls the ends of the third side outward. This is called tension. The forces of compression and tension are equal. The sides of the triangle evenly share weight. This keeps the shape stable.

Using a series of triangles adds more strength. They make a frame that supports a structure. This frame is called a truss. The Betsy Ross Bridge is a truss bridge. It spans the Delaware River between Pennsylvania and New Jersey. The bridge is made of steel.

History of the Truss

The idea of using trusses in buildings became popular in the early 1800s. Trusses were used to build bridges across waterways and canyons. These bridges allowed early US settlers to travel west in trains and wagons.

The triangles inside a truss bridge experience tension and compression. These forces hold the bridge steady.

Horizontal beams form the base and top of the truss. They are joined together with **diagonal** beams. These form triangles.

The triangles help **distribute** the forces pushing on the bridge. They make the bridge strong.

Engineers use arches and triangles in bridges, dams, and buildings. These shapes use compression and tension to stay strong. They transfer forces into solid ground. Arches and triangles create stable structures.

Explore Online

Visit the website below. Does it give any new information about triangles that wasn't in Chapter Three?

Strong Structures with Triangles

abdocorelibrary.com/arches-and-triangles-strong

Engineering Facts

Arch bridges compress when forces push down on top of them. They send the weight down to the base.

Roofs use triangles to distribute weight evenly.

Truss bridges use many triangles. These shapes give the bridges their strength.

Windows may be arched to stay strong under the weight of a building.

Glossary

beam
a long, straight piece of wood or metal

diagonal
related to a straight line joining two opposite corners of a straight-sided shape

distribute
to spread out

engineers
people who are trained to design and build machines and structures

force
a push or pull that transfers energy into an object

hinge
a device with a joint that can move

horizontal
related to a straight line that runs side to side

span
to stretch across

Online Resources

To learn more about triangles, visit our free resource websites below.

Visit **abdocorelibrary.com** or scan this QR code for free Common Core resources for teachers and students, including vetted activities, multimedia, and booklinks, for deeper subject comprehension.

Visit **abdobooklinks.com** or scan this QR code for free additional online weblinks for further learning. These links are routinely monitored and updated to provide the most current information available.

Learn More

Howell, Izzi. *Working with Buildings and Structures.* Kane Miller, 2022.

London, Martha. *Arches National Park.* Abdo, 2021.

Mattern, Joanne. *How Bridges Stand Strong.* Abdo, 2025.

Index

About the Author

Marne Ventura is the author of more than 150 books for children. She holds a master's degree in education from the University of California. She enjoys writing about STEM, arts and crafts, finance, people and places, food, and careers. Ventura and her family live in California.